MW00380288

Floral Stained Glass Lampshades

46 Full-Size Patterns

CONNIE CLOUGH EATON

Dover Publications, Inc.
New York

Copyright © 1990 by Connie Clough Eaton.
All rights reserved.

Floral Stained Glass Lampshades: 46 Full-Size Patterns is a new work,
first published by Dover Publications, Inc., in 1990.

Library of Congress Cataloging-in-Publication Data

Eaton, Connie.
    Floral stained glass lampshades : 46 full-size patterns / Connie
Clough Eaton.
        p.   cm.
  ISBN-13: 978-0-486-26278-9
  ISBN-10: 0-486-26278-2
    1. Glass craft. 2. Glass painting and staining—Patterns.
3. Flowers in art. I. Title.
TT298.E175 1990
749'.63—dc20   89-26024
                                                    CIP

Manufactured in the United States by LSC Communications
26278212   2017
www.doverpublications.com

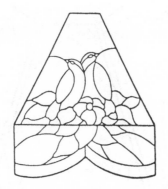

INTRODUCTION

This book contains full-size patterns for making 46 lampshades. Stained glass lampshades of this type were first made by Louis C. Tiffany at the turn of the century, and have since become valuable and cherished heirlooms. These projects are intended for the craftsperson already familiar with the basics of the craft, so instructions on such skills as selecting and cutting glass are not provided here. Those not familiar with these skills are referred to one of the many introductions to stained glass currently available (among the best is *Stained Glass Craft* by J. A. F. Divine and G. Blachford, Dover Publications, 0-486-22812-6).

Each assembled lampshade may have 4, 6 or 8 sides, depending on how large and elaborate you want the finished lampshade to be. Some lampshades have angle pieces that fit on the bottom; these require a slightly more complicated assembly. Some patterns, for space reasons, have their top sections separated—don't forget to add them back in when working on the lampshades.

How to Use the Patterns

Trace the desired pattern from the book onto heavyweight paper. This tracing will then be used as a template. It is important to keep the edges of the heavyweight paper as neat and firm as possible, so use very sharp scissors or an X-Acto knife when cutting out a template. The original pattern from the book is then used as a reference when the time comes to assemble the pieces to form a lampshade panel. Number the pieces on the template and on the tracing.

Copper Foil Technique

Begin by assembling the individual panels using the copper foil technique. Use adhesive-backed copper foil, which is available in 36-yard rolls, in widths of ³⁄₁₆″, ¼″, ⅜″ and ½″. After cutting the glass, wrap a thin strip of foil around the edges of each piece. Make certain that the glass is centered over the foil so that it extends an equal distance on both sides of the glass. The foil strip should be long enough to go around all edges of the piece and overlap itself by about ¼″. Press the foil carefully and firmly into place using a fid, burnisher or pencil. Trim excess foil at the corners with a scissor, razor blade or X-Acto knife.

Fit the glass pieces of an individual panel together, treating any pieces which are to hang off the bottom as separate units. Tack the corners of each piece of glass by holding a soldering iron or gun over the corners and dropping a piece of solder onto the corner. Coat the foil with a thin layer of flux and then move the soldering gun along the foil while pulling the solder close behind. On contact with the foil, the solder should melt and spread out along the entire width of the foil. Repeat this procedure with the other panels.

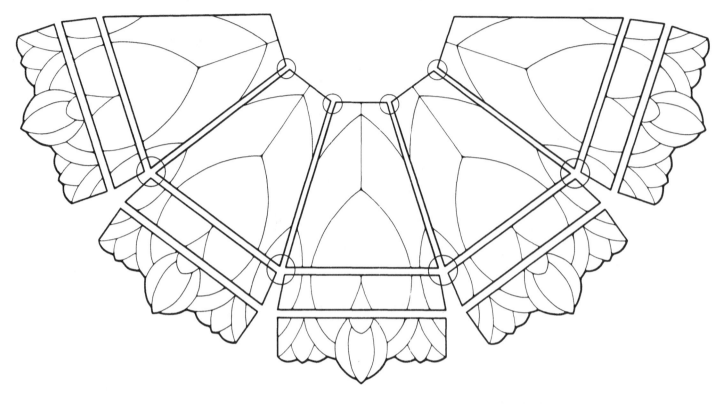

Figure 1

Assembling the Lampshade

Place all completed panels *face down* and edge-to-edge, as in figure 1. Tack the panels together at the points indicated by the circles, using small drops of solder. Tack the hanging panel(s) to the bottom of the main panel using a bead of solder at each corner. *Do not* tack the sides of the hanging panels to each other at this time, but leave them splayed out from the main panels. Very carefully, turn the lampshade *face up*.

Grasp the two unattached sides of the assembly and bring them up so that the two edges meet and the lampshade assumes the familiar circular shape. Tack the free ends together on the outside with two drops of solder.

The hanging pieces can now be pushed into place, so that their adjacent edges meet, and form tiers at a different angle than the main part of the shade. Tack adjacent hanging sections at the corners.

In the same way that you soldered individual pieces together to form panels, solder all panels and hanging sections together, first on the outside, then on the inside of the lampshade. The lampshade should rest on its topside as you solder the inside, and on its bottom as you solder the outside.

Visit your local hardware or electrical supply store to see the electrical fixtures that are available and for information on how to install them. Because the shades are quite heavy, they are more suitable for hanging lamps than for table lamps.

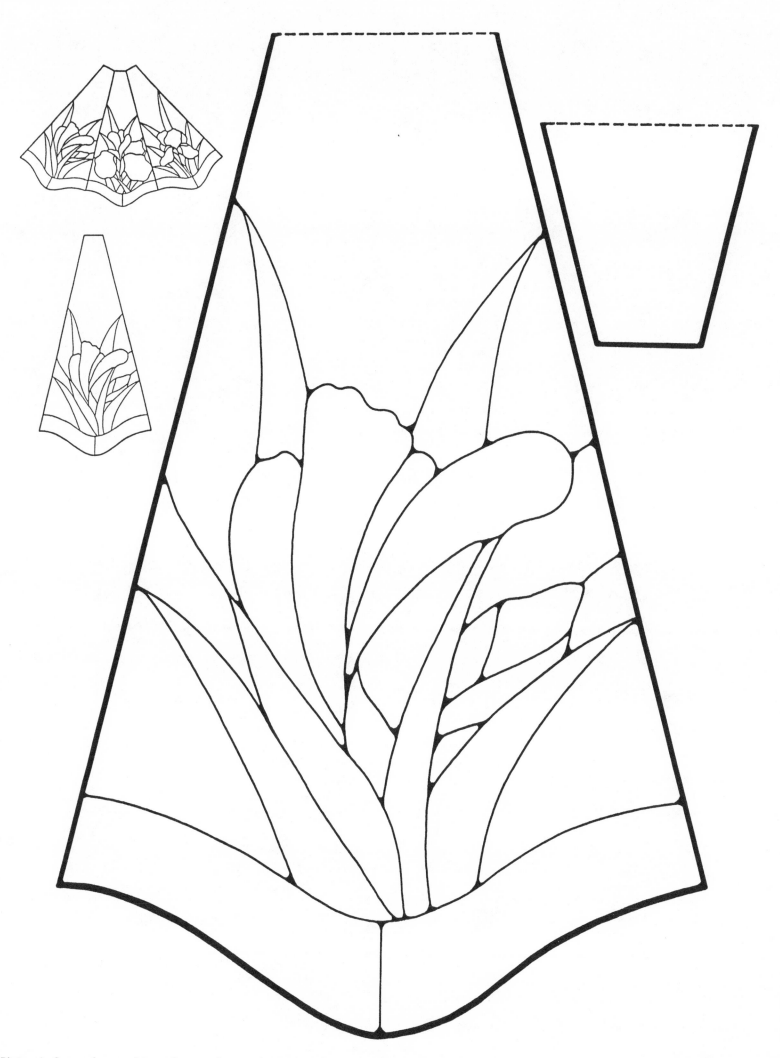

Plates 1–3 may be used together as shown above.

PLATE 1

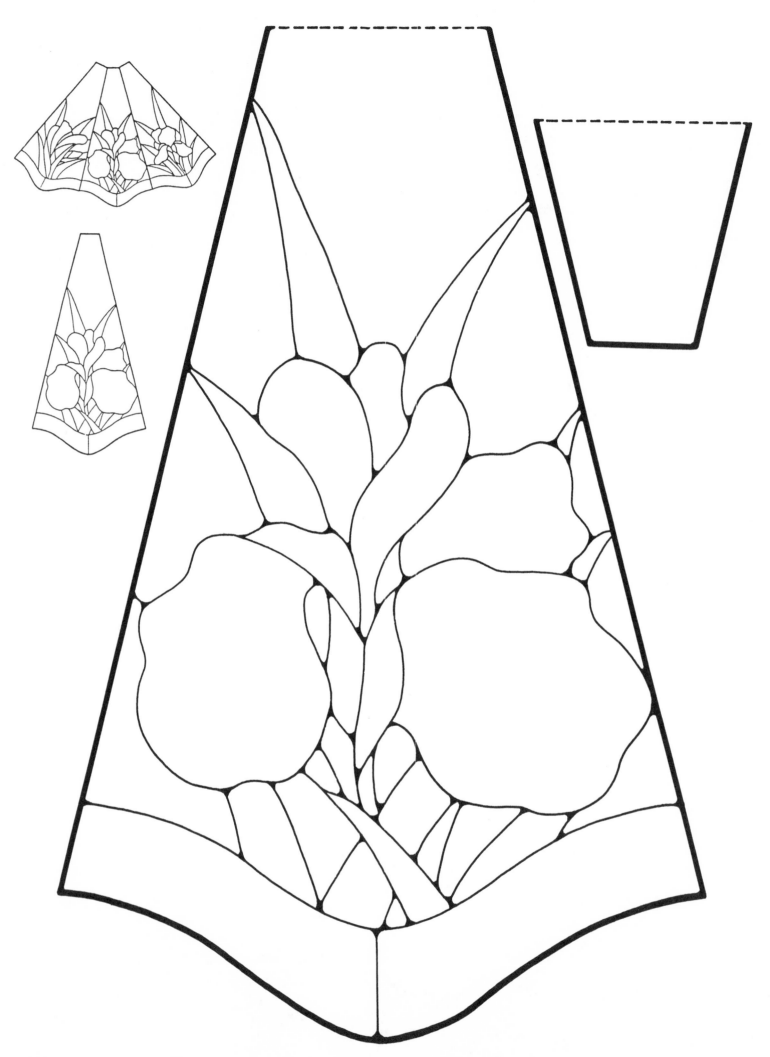

PLATE 2

PLATE 3

PLATE 4

Plates 4–6 may be used together as shown above.

PLATE 5

PLATE 6

PLATE 7

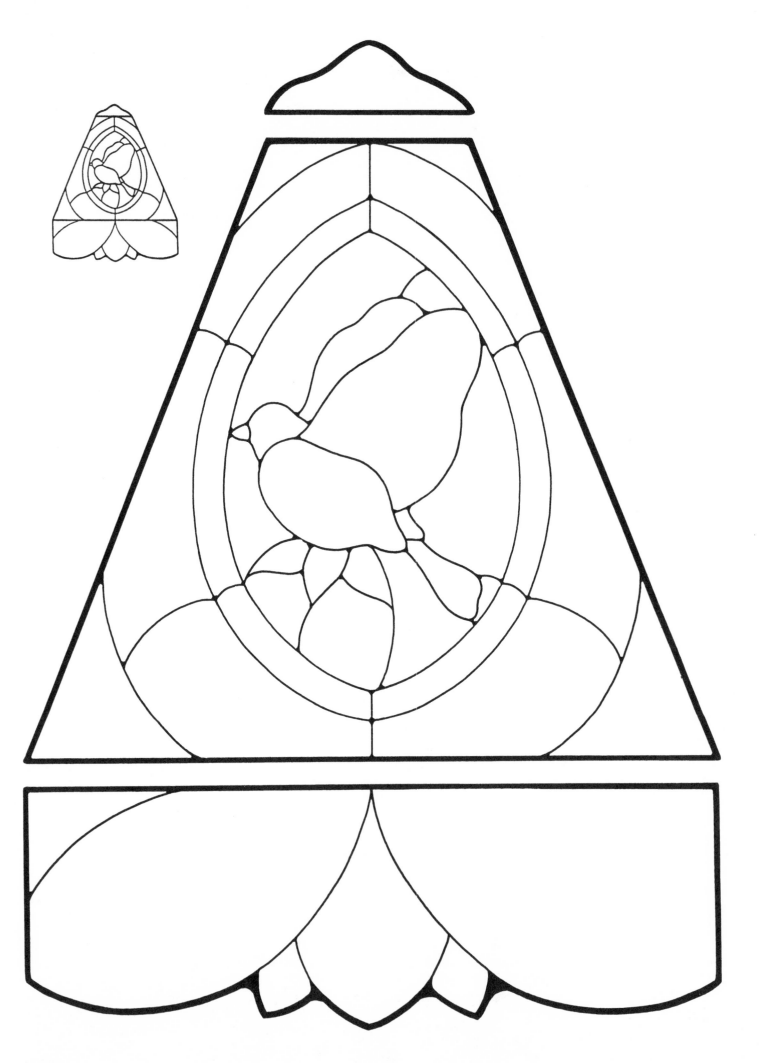

PLATE 8

PLATE 9

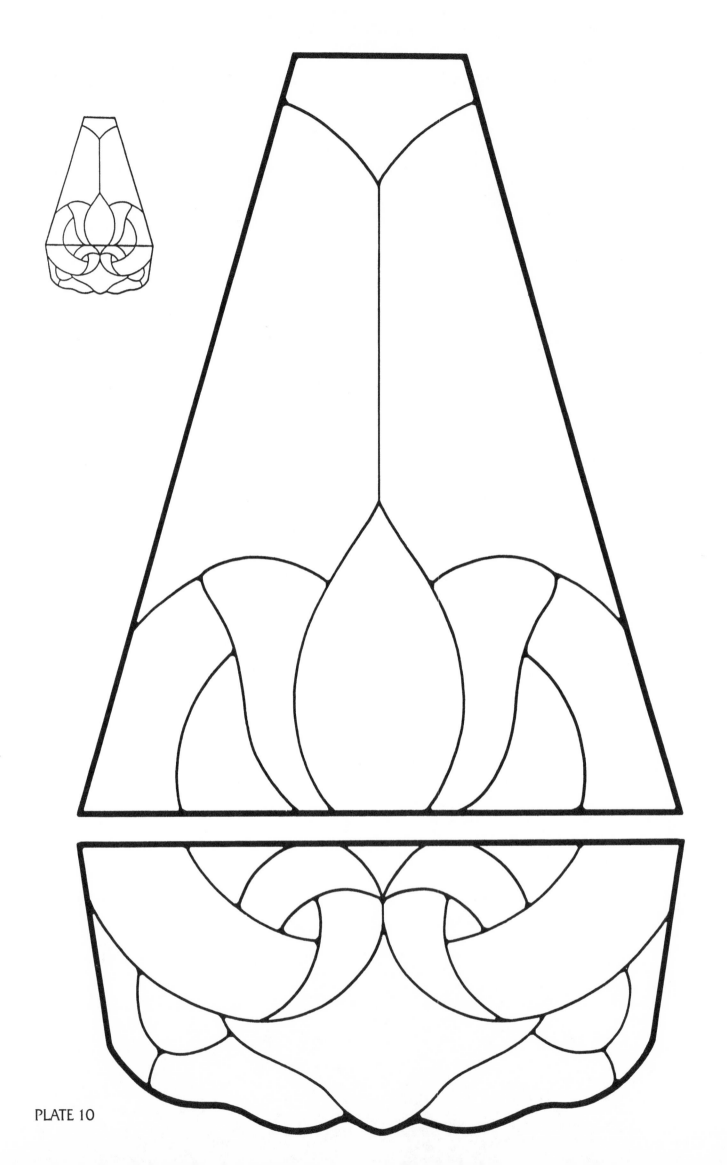

PLATE 10

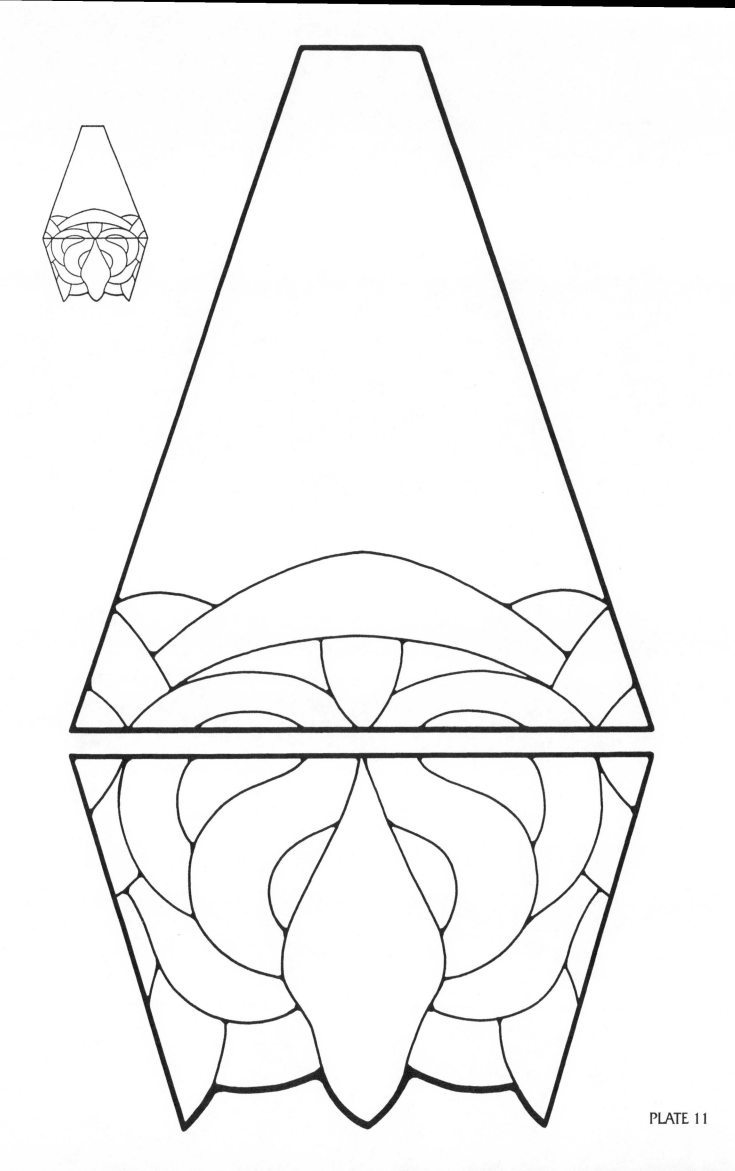

PLATE 11

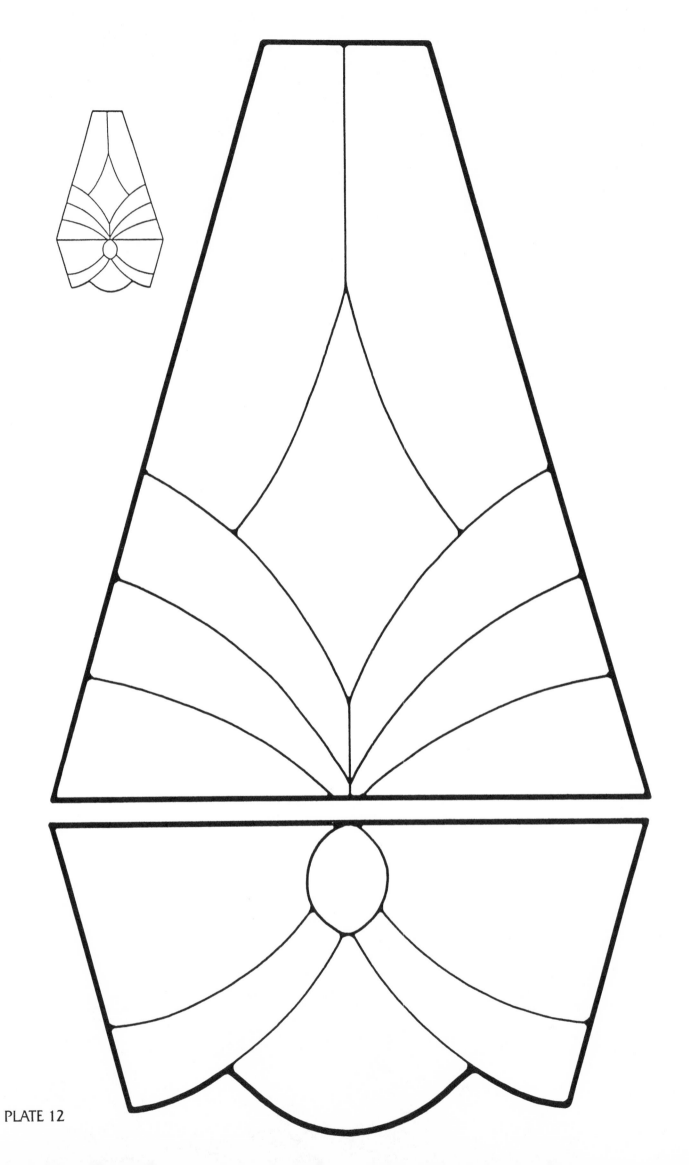

PLATE 12

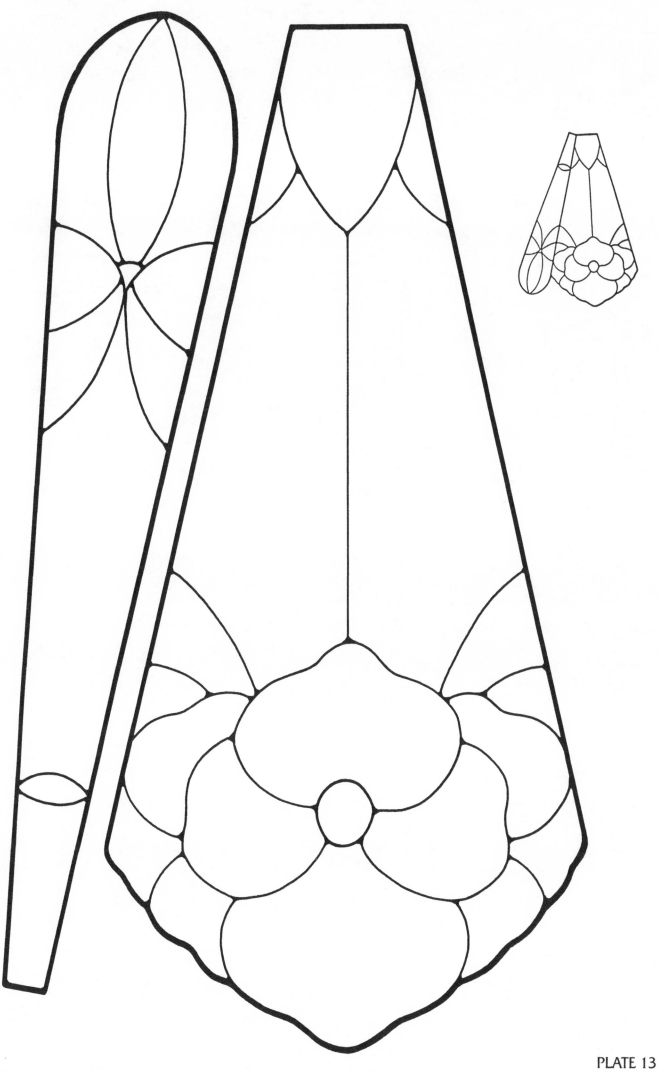

PLATE 13

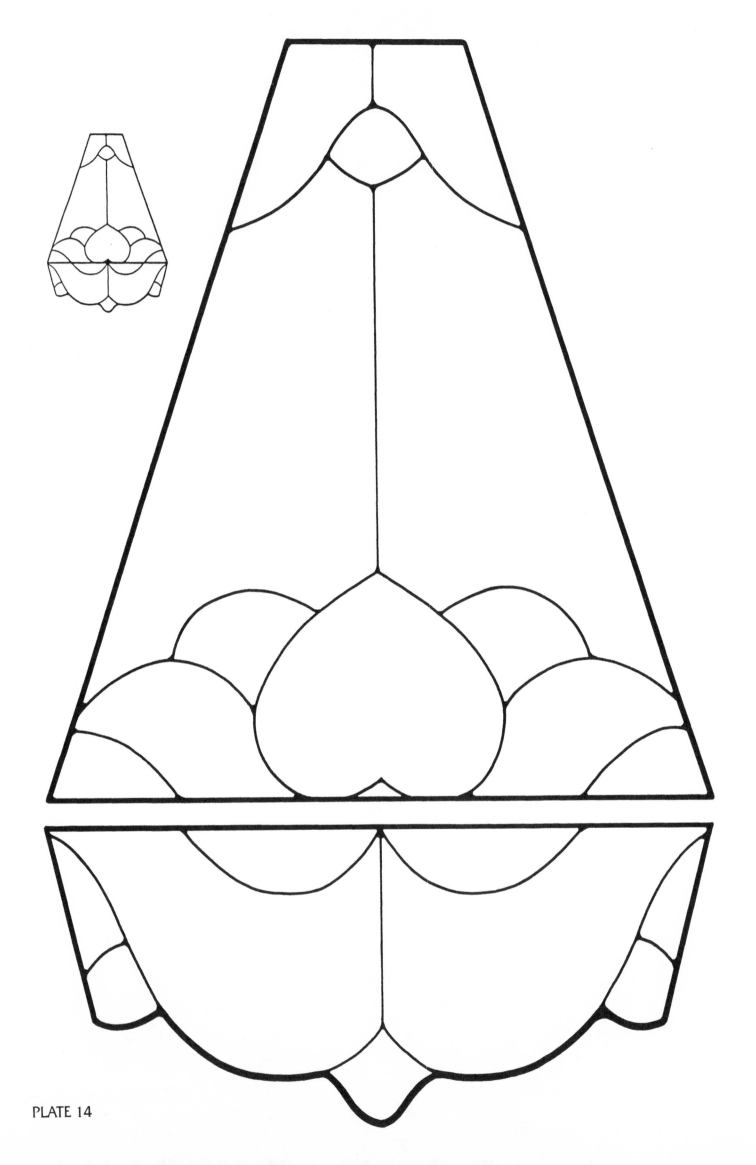

PLATE 14

PLATE 15

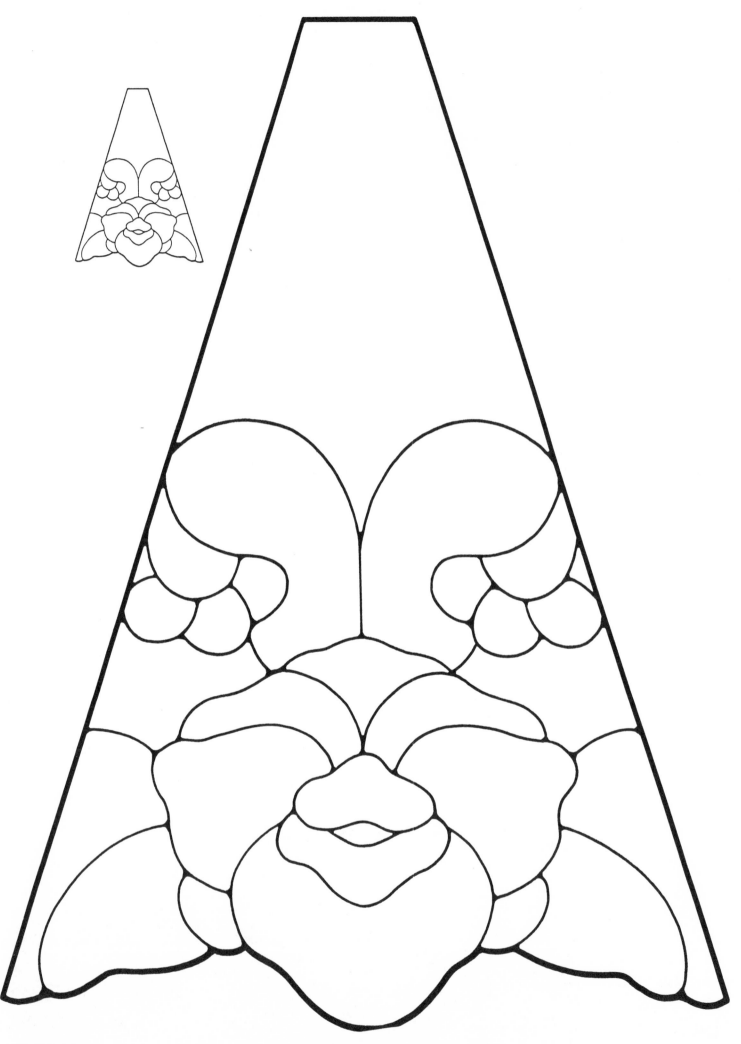

PLATE 16

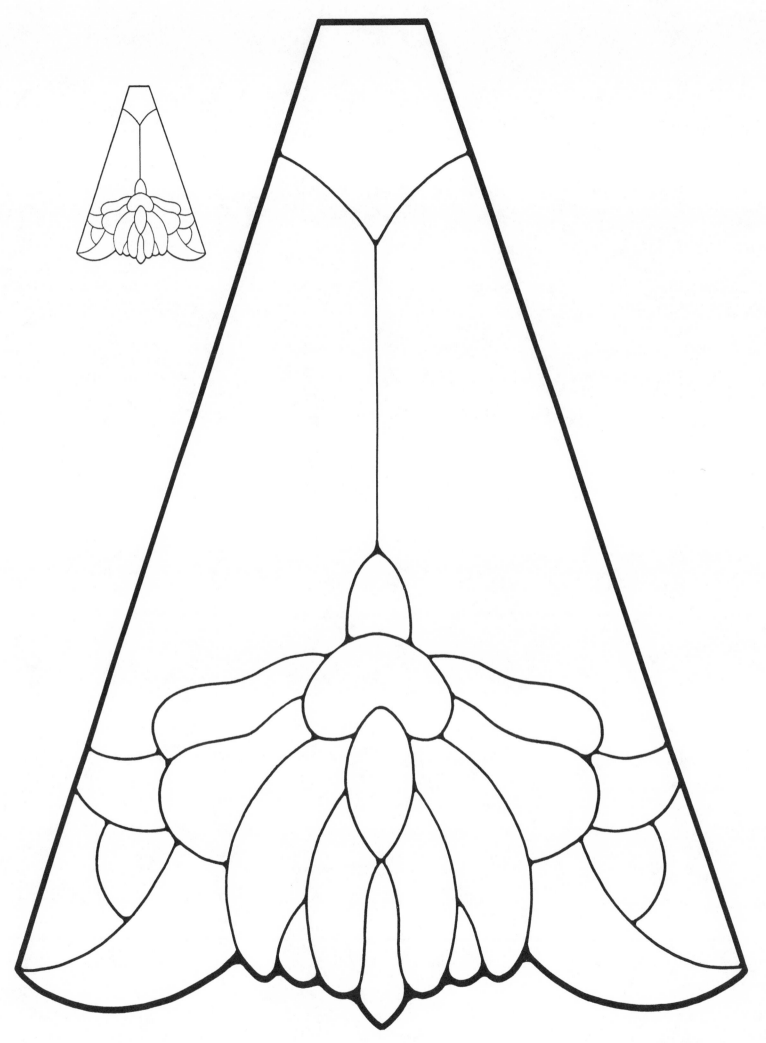

PLATE 17

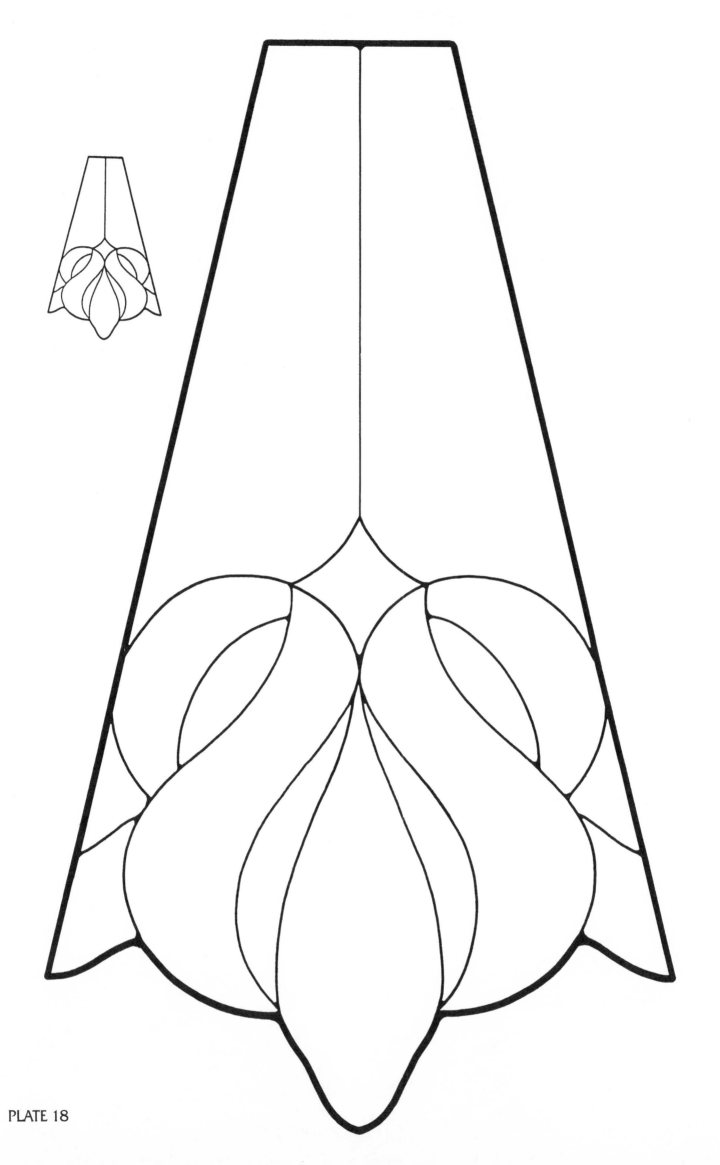

PLATE 18

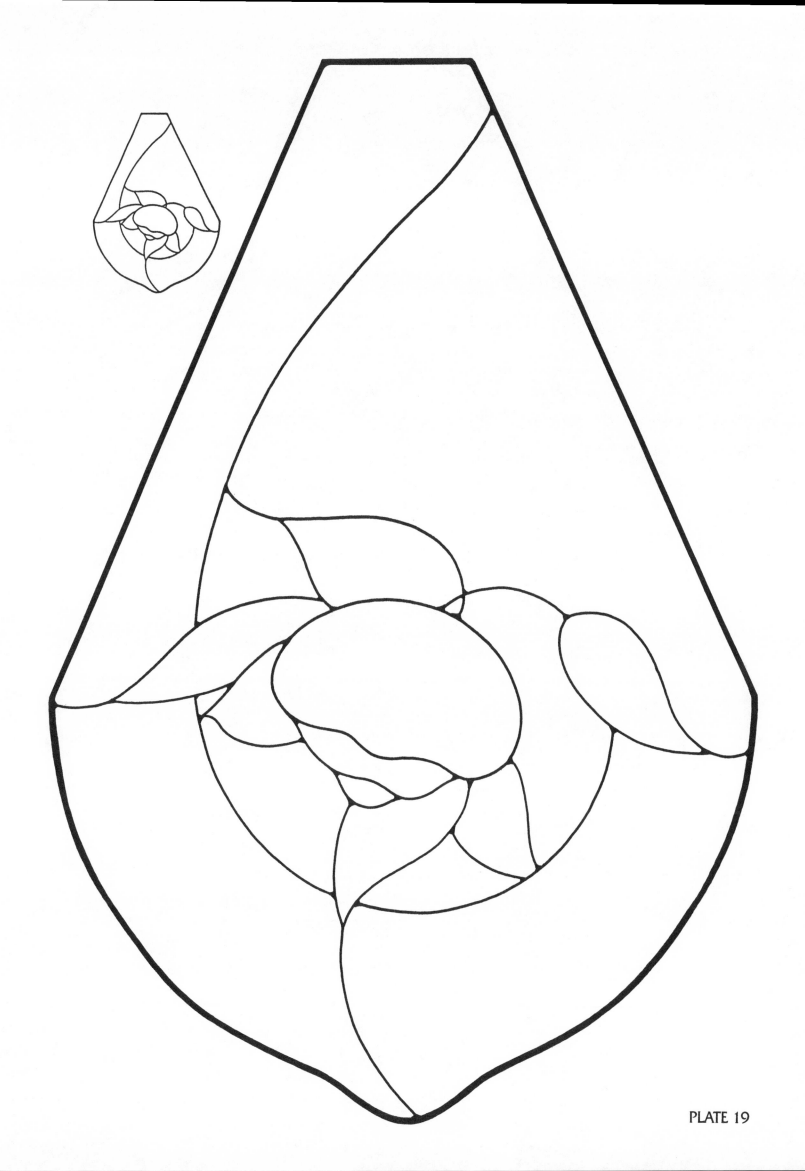

PLATE 19

PLATE 20

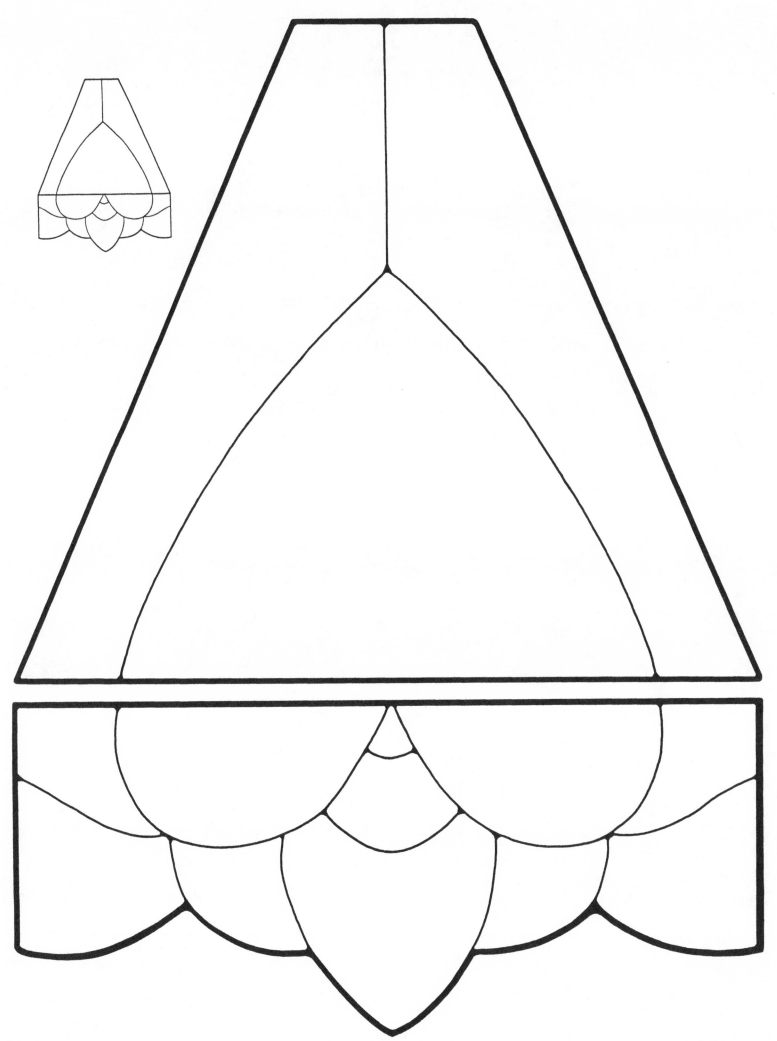

PLATE 21

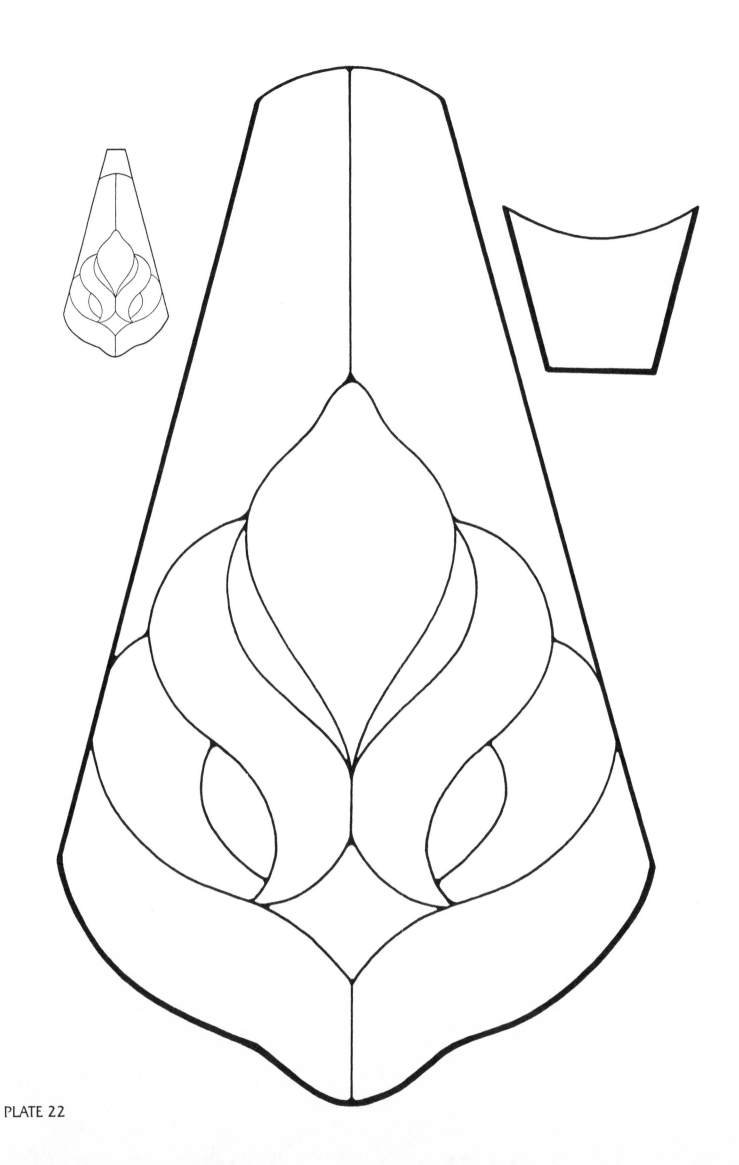

PLATE 22

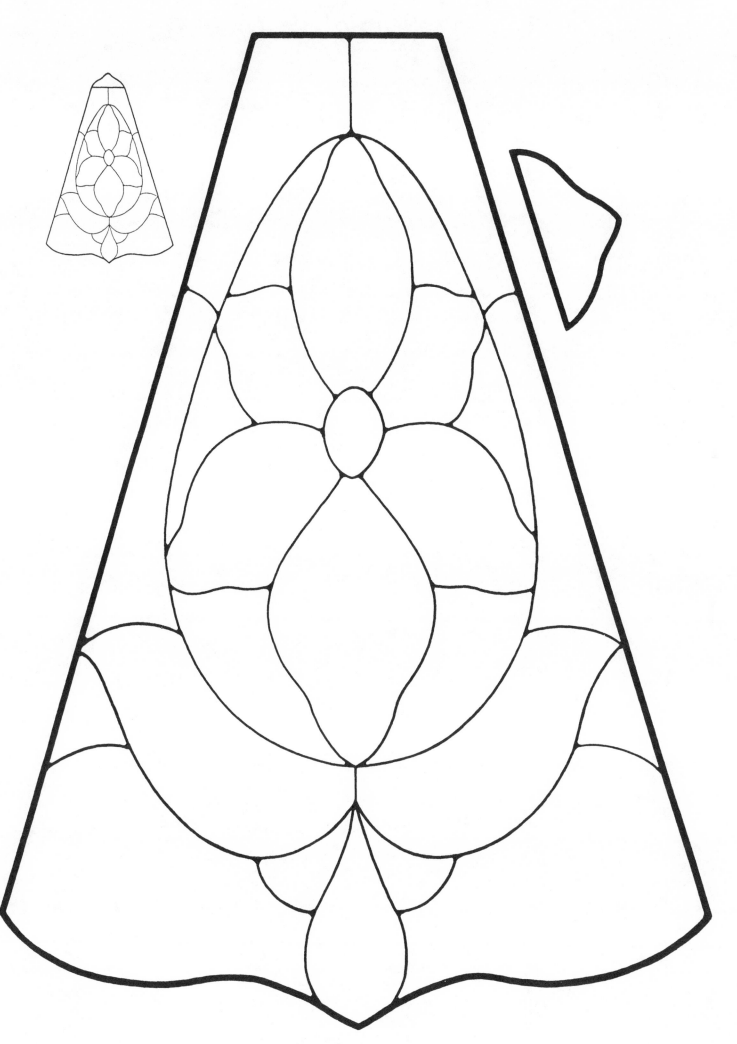

PLATE 23

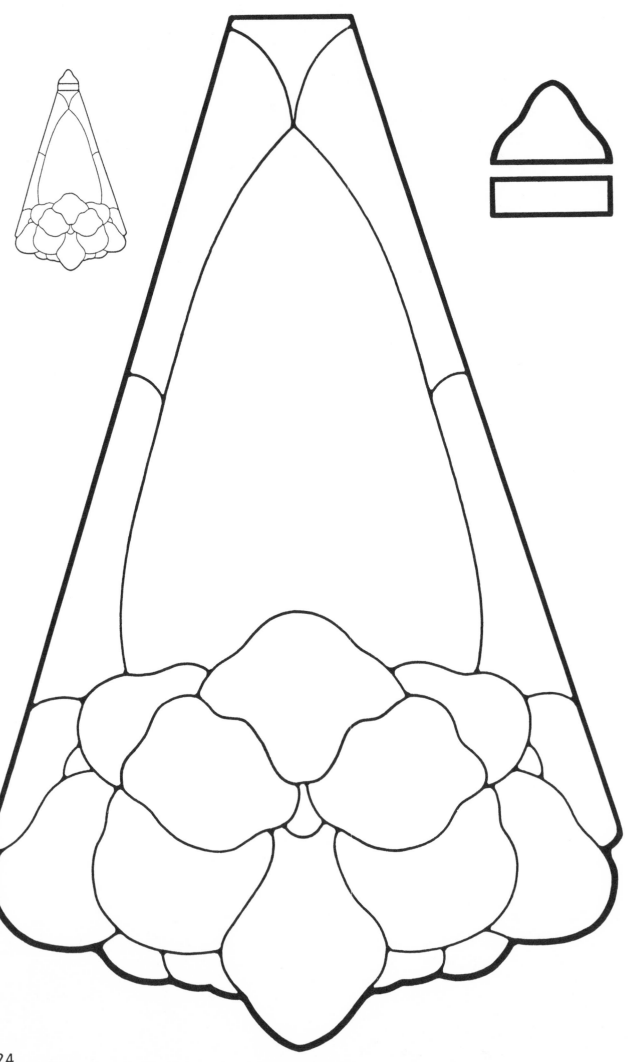

PLATE 24

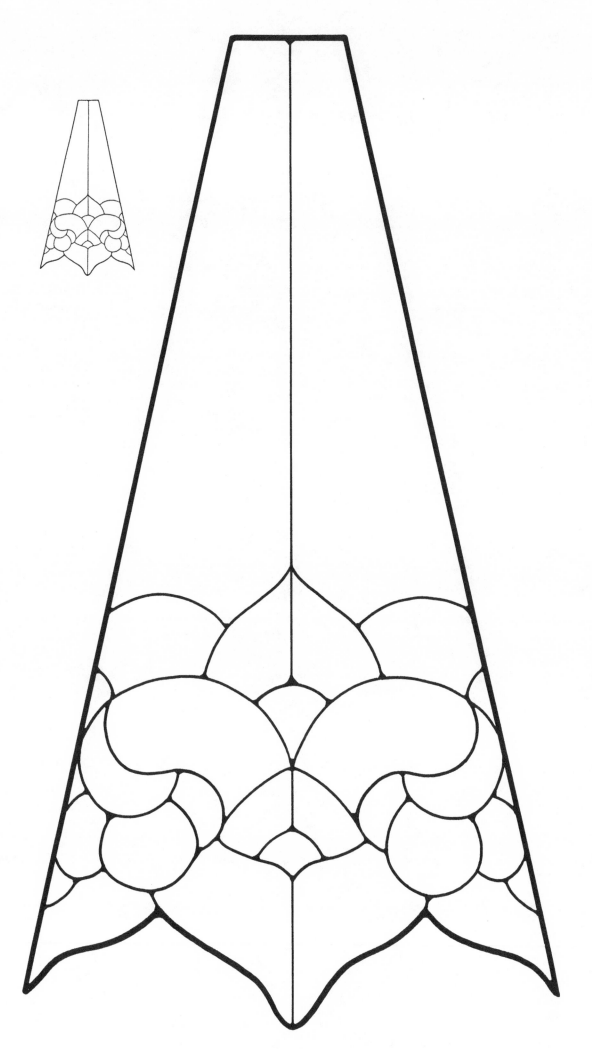

PLATE 25

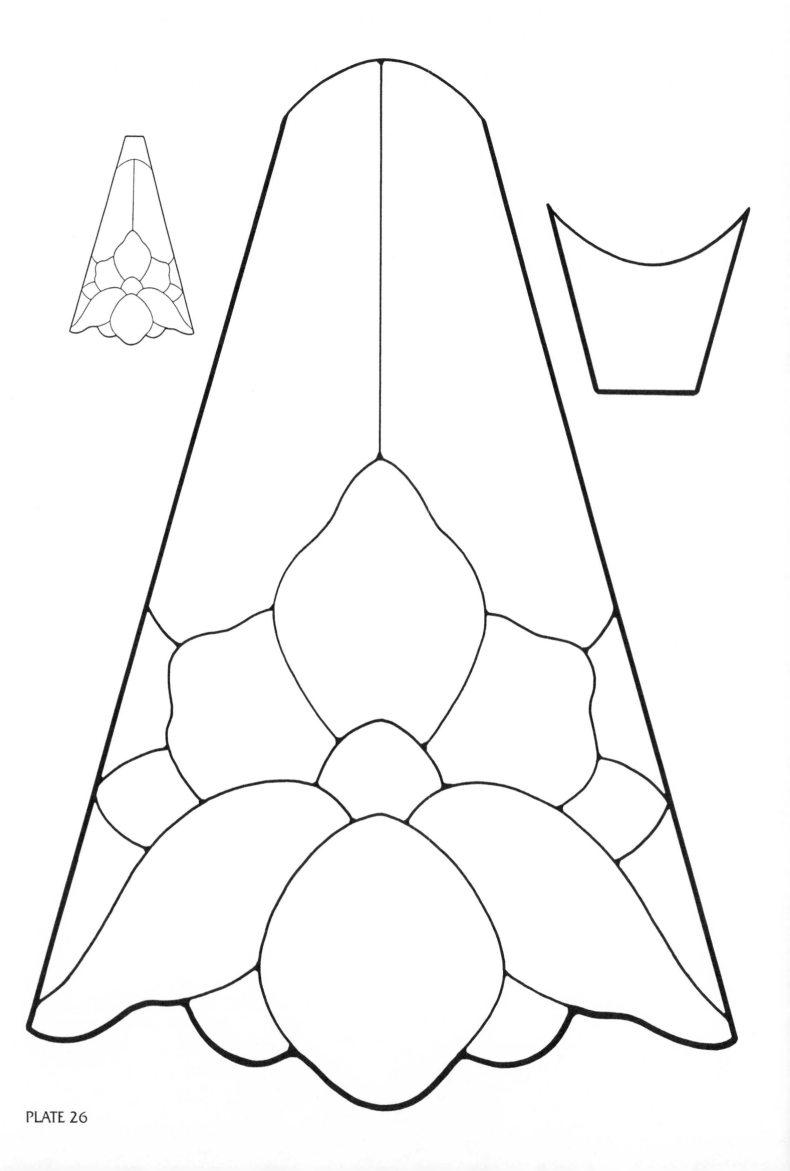

PLATE 26

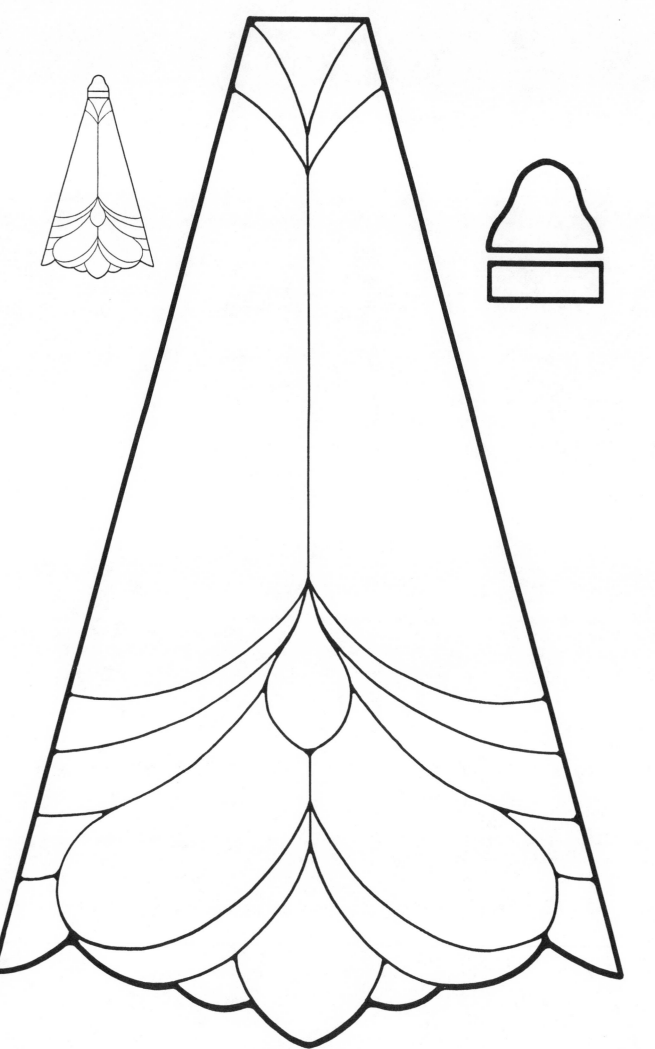

PLATE 27

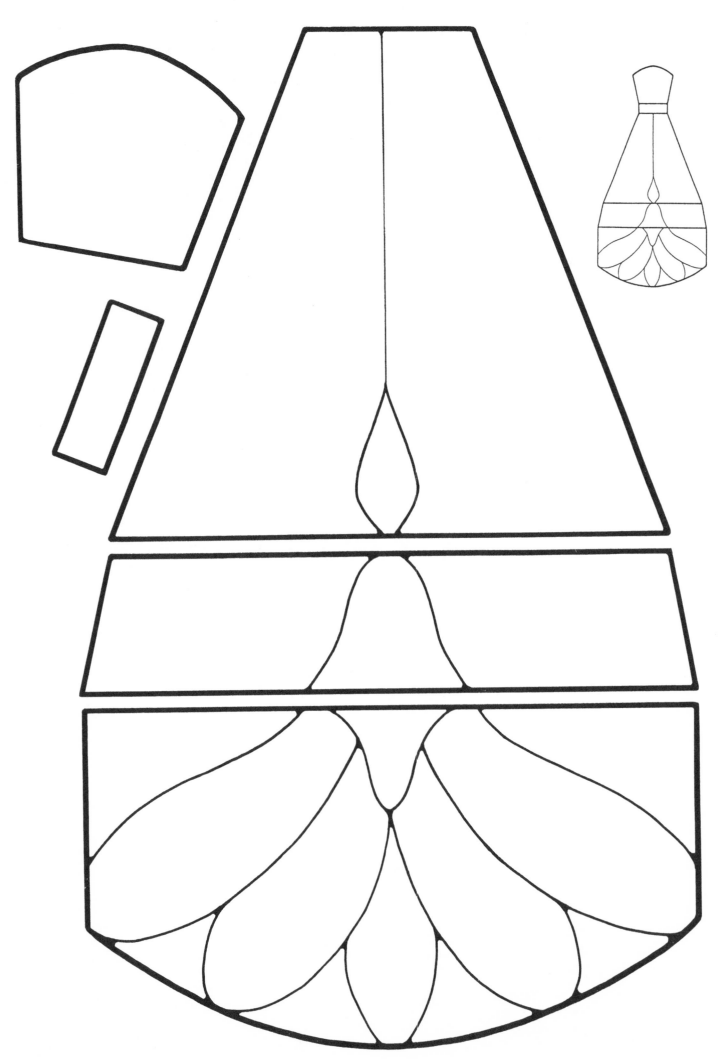

PLATE 28

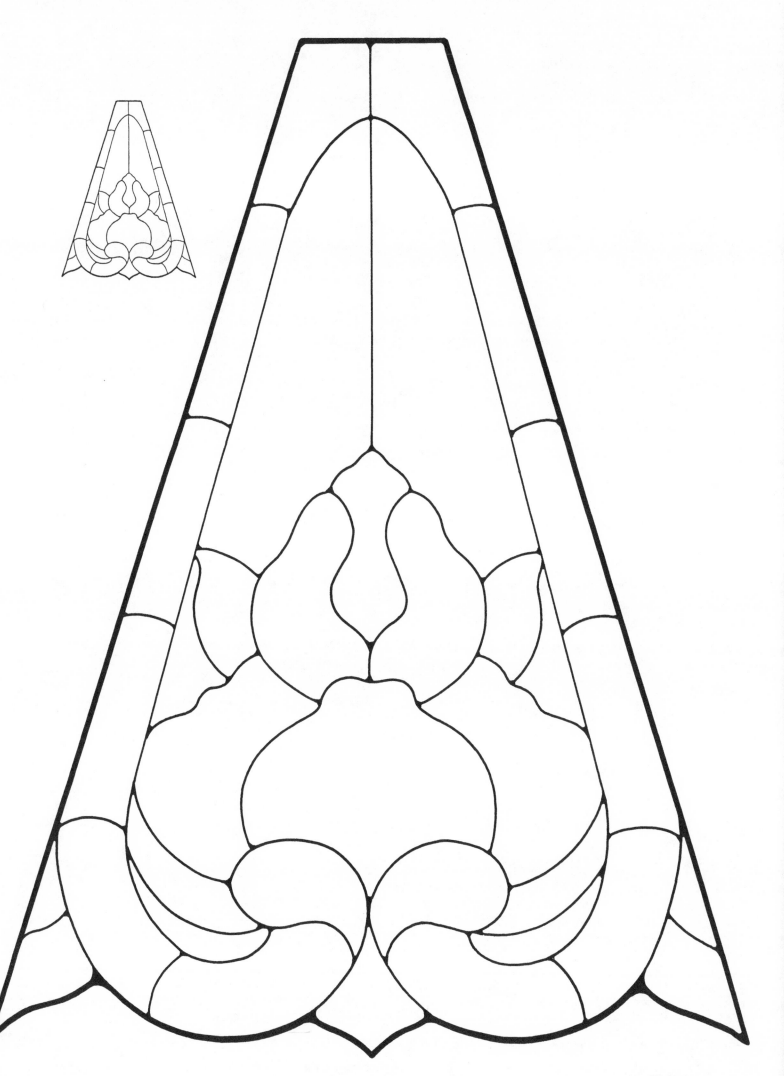

PLATE 29

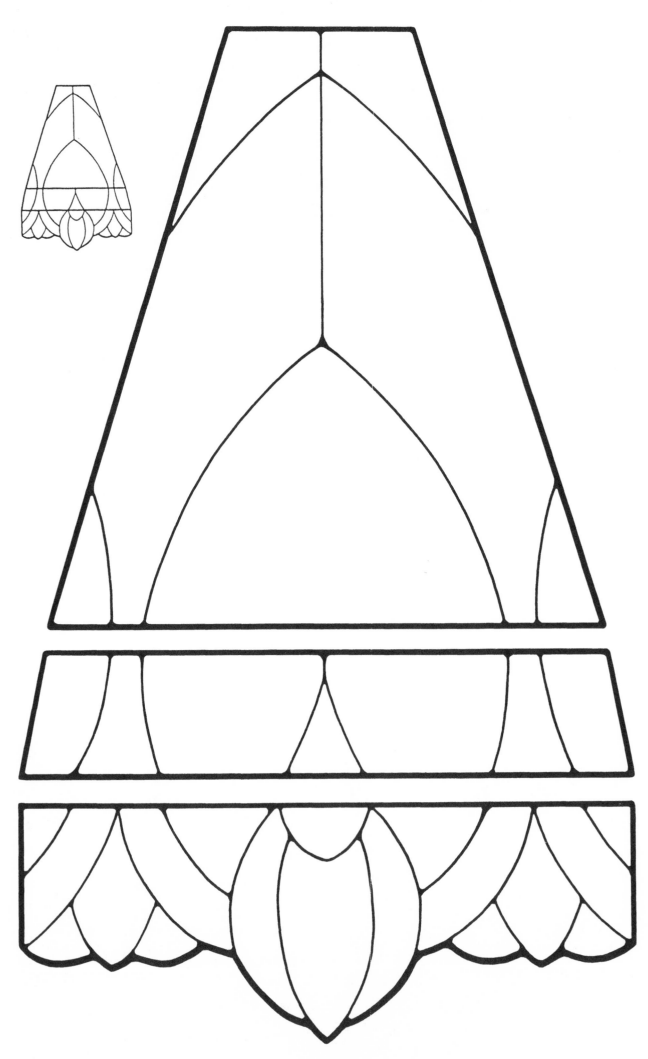

PLATE 30

PLATE 31

PLATE 33

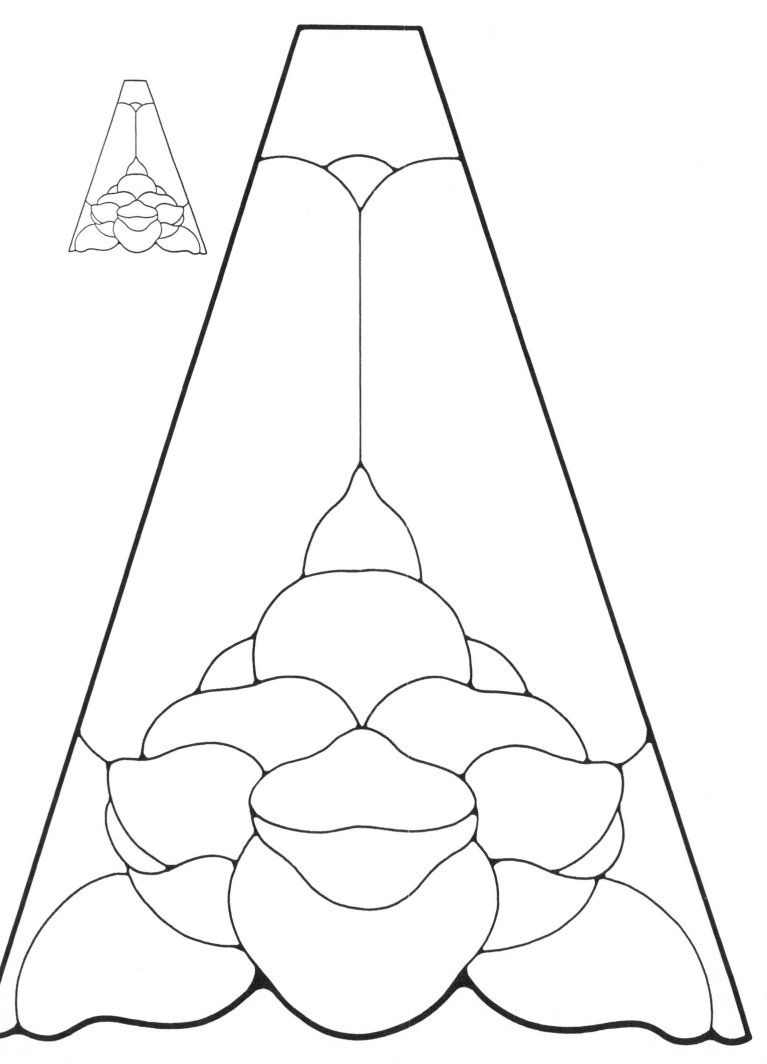

PLATE 34

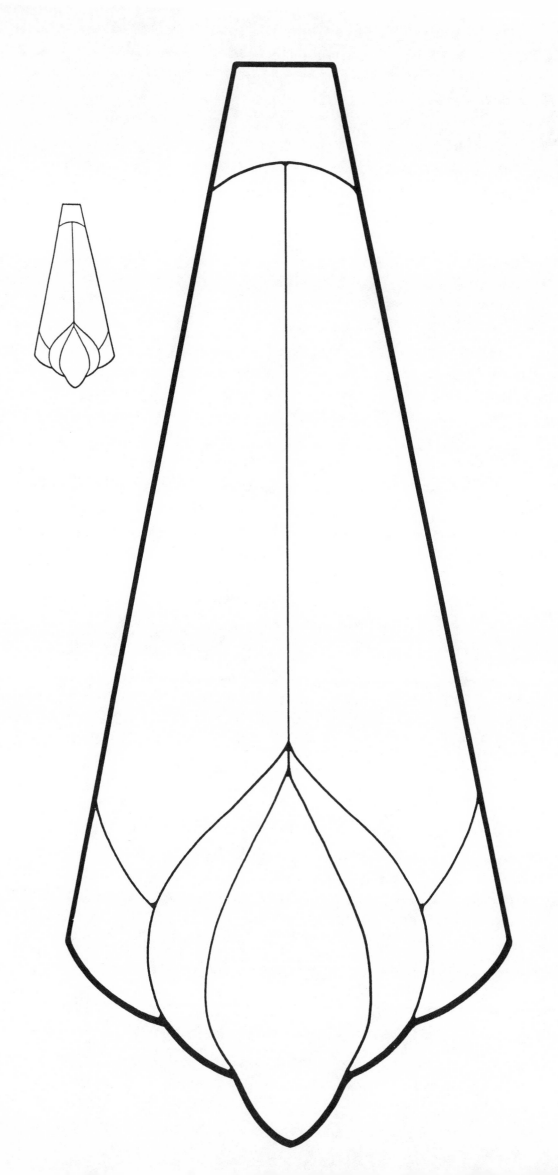

PLATE 35

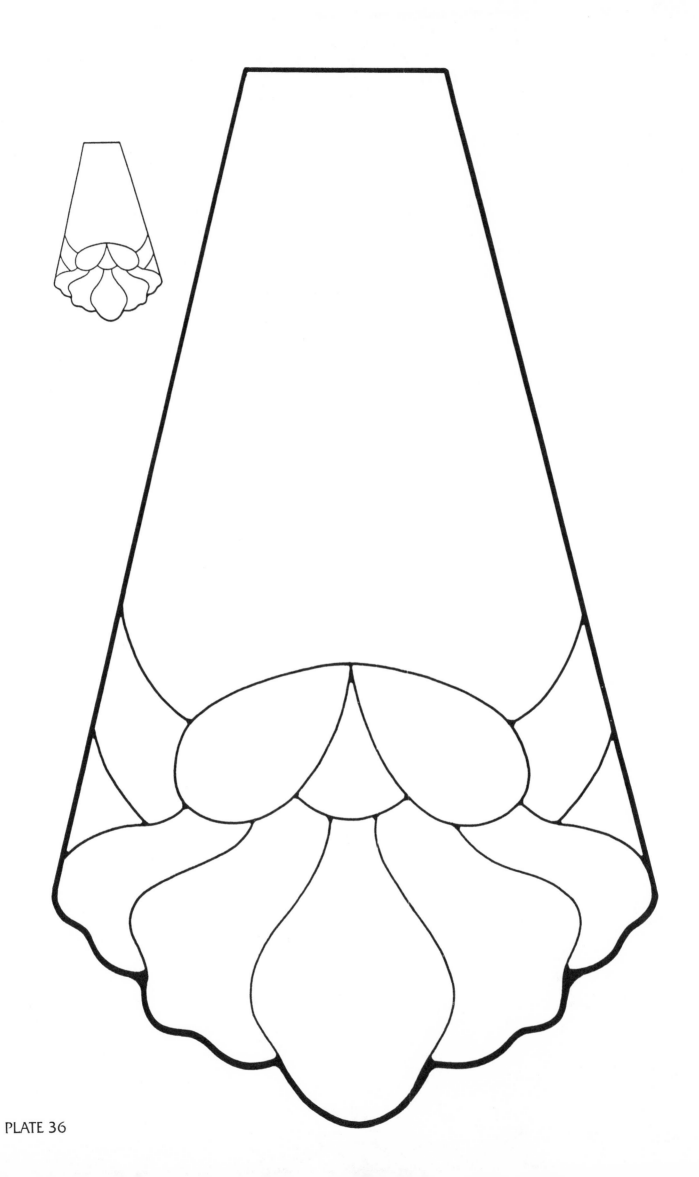

PLATE 36

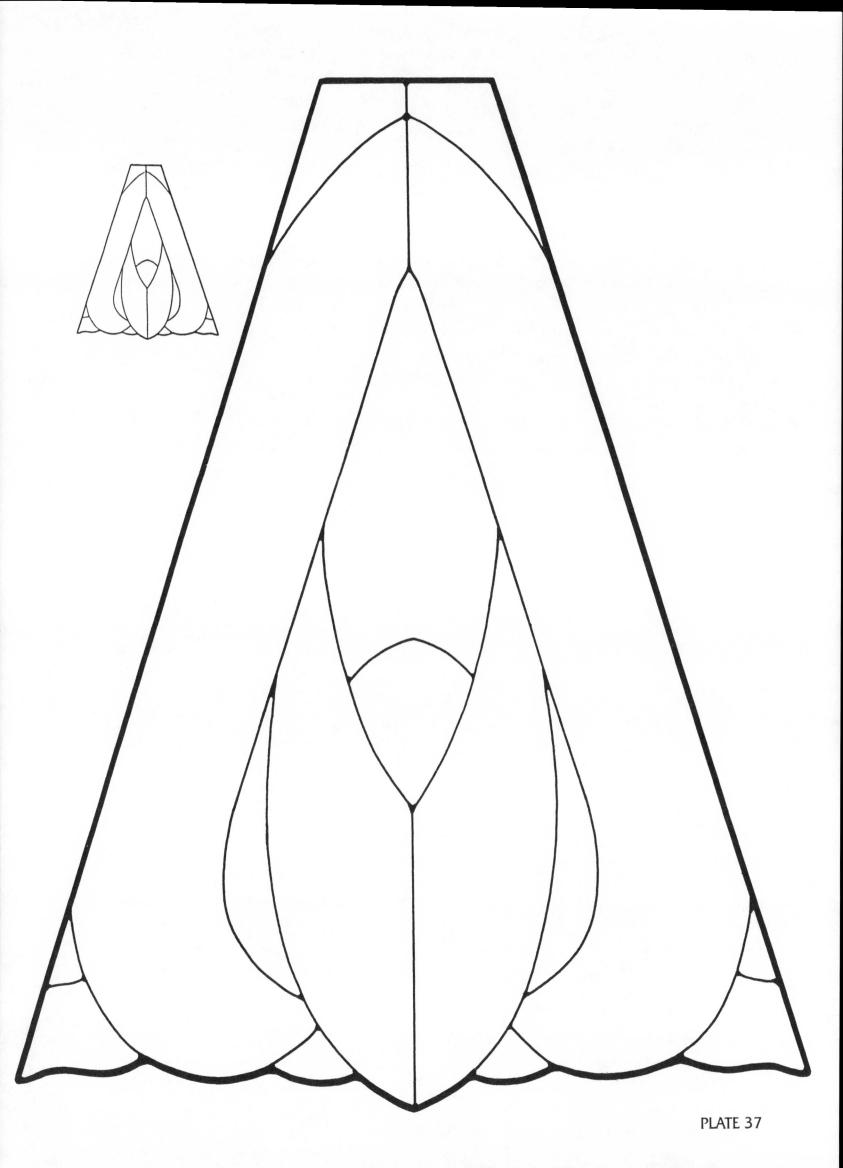

PLATE 37

PLATE 38

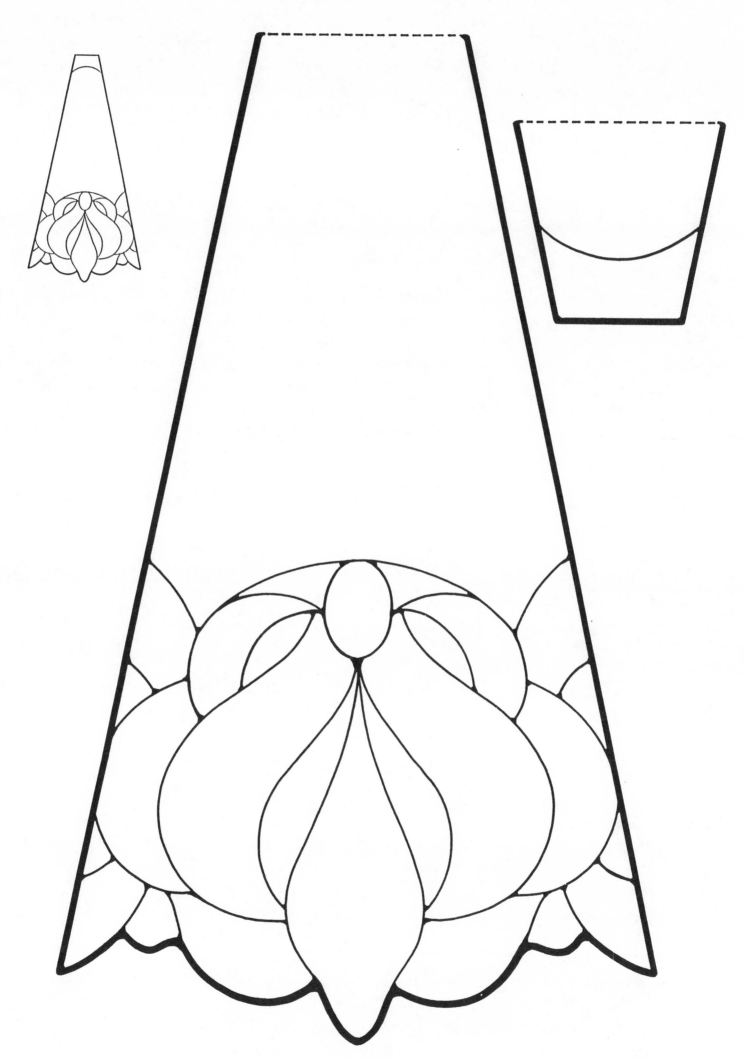

PLATE 39

PLATE 41

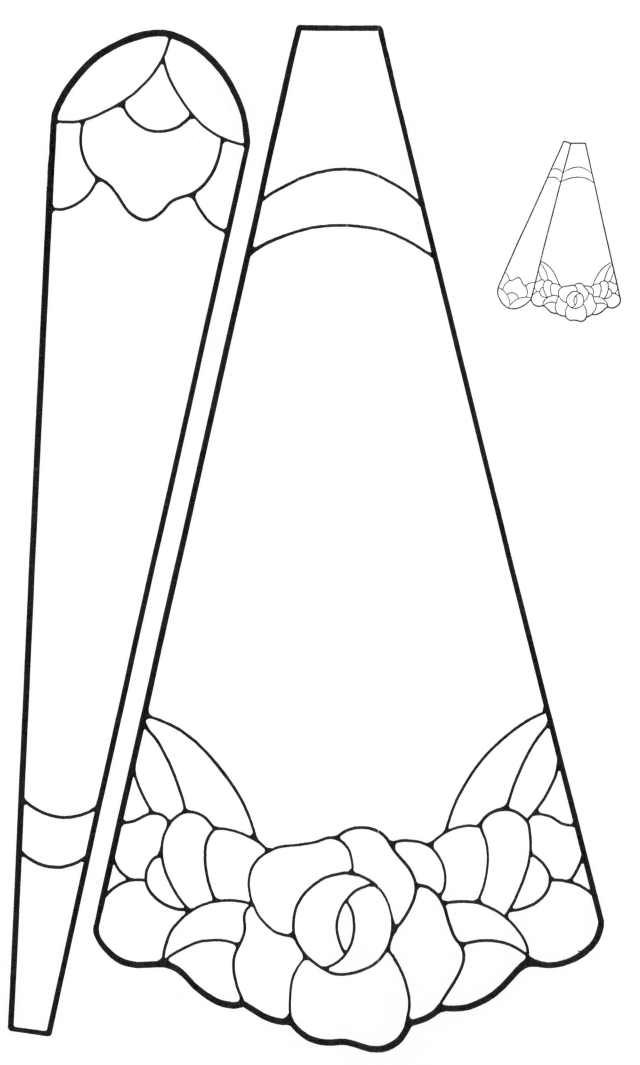

PLATE 42

PLATE 43

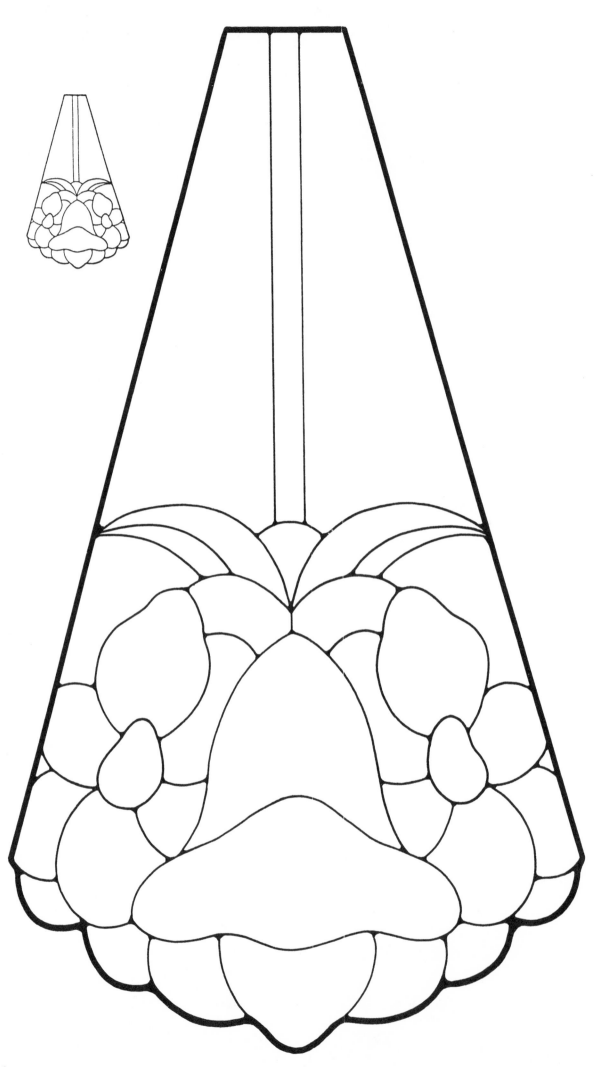

PLATE 44

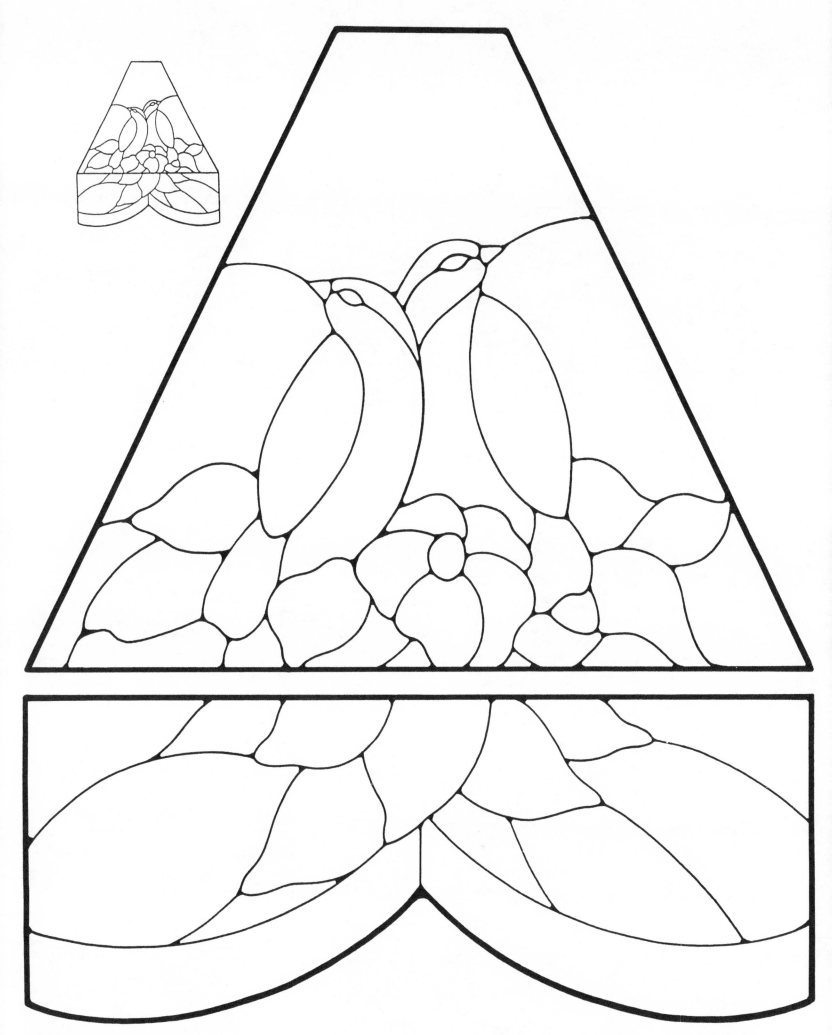

PLATE 45

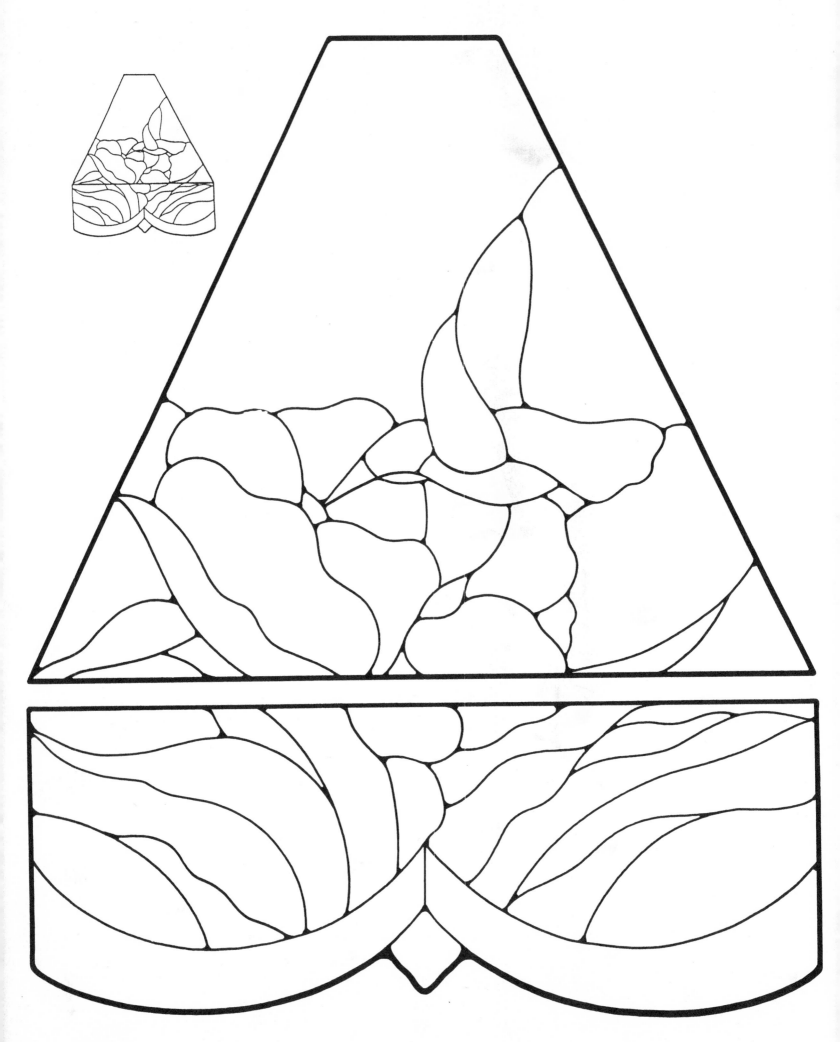

PLATE 46